My Shining Moments Journal

My Shining Moments Journal

Margaret Cook, M.Ed., L.P.C.
Licensed Professional Counselor
Life Coach
Book Coach

Published by All She Writ Publishing, LLC

ISBN: 978-0-9886902-5-7

Printed in the United States of America

Introduction

Your day has many experiences. Those experiences involve emotions and thoughts about your life. Positive Psychology research indicates that if you notice the good things and feelings, you may experience a sense of well-being, increased satisfaction and, ultimately, happiness.

Cultivating habits or patterns of behavior that help you look for the good may increase the likelihood that things you enjoy will happen more often. This journal is an exercise in noticing the shining moments of each day. You will have a space to write three experiences. On the opposite page, you will have space to reflect about the experiences. Once a week there is a BONUS set of pages. The BONUS is an opportunity that you make to share your appreciation or experience with someone else.

It is great to be spontaneous and not overthink the daily entries. You may list little joys or moments that were stunning for you. Even noticing the small positives is an important practice in cultivating a sense of feeling thankful.

You may notice things about yourself. For example, moments when you do/say/think/feel something that uses your strengths or appreciates your vulnerability. You may notice things about others and how they make a difference in your day. Noticing and expressing these experiences to someone else is a way of building connections. When people feel connected to each other, they are able to care and to help foster strength and resilience. The BONUS weekly exercise of sharing may become one of the great joys of practicing daily appreciation.

Three Moments

Set aside a few minutes (maybe five to ten) each day to write in this journal. On the left side of the book is a page with three blocks. In each block, write a sentence or phrase about something good that happened in the last 24 hours. Think about anything that happened, or that you thought or heard about that prompted you to feel thankful or grateful.

Write enough to be meaningful to you. Some writers just need a few words to describe the experience. Others like to write descriptively about each shining moment.

You may have a variety of things that inspire you to notice something good. Maybe a special song came on when you started the car. Perhaps you asked a good question in class or understood something new. It may have been a few moments outdoors when you noticed the weather, sunshine or beauty in your surroundings. Maybe you were able to help or encourage someone or maybe someone special reached out to you and made a difference. Whatever caused a feeling of appreciation would be something to list on this page.

Reflection

What made that moment shine for you? Use the right side of the page to reflect on the item on the facing page. What made the experience special or memorable? Why did this experience happen? Are there things you might do that would cultivate having positive experiences like that again or more often? Does the experience remind you of other moments or people?

Take a few minutes to make meaning of the shining moments of your day. Reflecting helps you become more aware of yourself in a healthy way. It helps you understand what encourages and inspires you. Reflecting may be like looking in the mirror and seeing who you are. This practice may be helpful for a variety of life experiences. In this journal, it will help you grow in your appreciation for the shining moments of your life each day.

Bonus

Gratitude reaches a new level and may multiply your appreciation exponentially when you share your experience with someone else.

In this journal there is a section, after every seven days, to prompt you to share a shining moment with someone else. You may share it with a stranger or with someone you know. What you share and how you engage with the other person is something you may do creatively. Maybe you will want to send a THANK YOU text or note to someone that was involved in a shining moment from your week. Maybe you want to call or visit with someone and talk about a special memory or acknowledge something you appreciate about that person. You may even engage in some "random act of kindness." Take action and share positivity in some way that is meaningful for you.

Use the journal pages to write what you did and how the other person responded. On the facing page reflect on why it was meaningful or on what else you may want to do to share your appreciation in the future. The reflection page is where you step back and look at the experience and write about the meaning of it for you. You may even ask the other person/people what your action meant to them.

Try to use this journal consistently for thirty days. You may be surprised at the number of shining moments you are experiencing. Shine on!

Week: _____ Date: _____

Three shining moments of this day

1. giving my band tutor
   a gift
   _____
   _____
   _____
   _____

2. Kaitlyn joining Pt
   _____
   _____
   _____
   _____

3. I looked really good today
   _____
   _____
   _____
   _____
   _____

Reflecting on my shining moments

1. _____

_____

_____

_____

_____

_____

2. _____

_____

_____

_____

_____

_____

3. _____

_____

_____

_____

_____

_____

Week: _____ Date: _____

Three shining moments of this day

1. _____
   _____
   _____
   _____
   _____
   _____

2. _____
   _____
   _____
   _____
   _____
   _____

3. _____
   _____
   _____
   _____
   _____
   _____

Reflecting on my shining moments

1. _____

_____

_____

_____

_____

_____

2. _____

_____

_____

_____

_____

3. _____

_____

_____

_____

_____

Week: _____   Date: _____

Three shining moments of this day

1. _____

_____

_____

_____

_____

_____

_____

2. _____

_____

_____

_____

_____

_____

_____

3. _____

_____

_____

_____

_____

_____

_____

Reflecting on my shining moments

1. _____

2. _____

3. _____

Three shining moments of this day

1. _____

_____

_____

_____

_____

_____

2. _____

_____

_____

_____

_____

_____

3. _____

_____

_____

_____

_____

_____

Reflecting on my shining moments

1. _____

_____

_____

_____

_____

_____

_____

2. _____

_____

_____

_____

_____

_____

_____

3. _____

_____

_____

_____

_____

_____

_____

Week: _____ Date: _____

Three shining moments of this day

1. _____
_____
_____
_____
_____
_____
_____

2. _____
_____
_____
_____
_____
_____
_____

3. _____
_____
_____
_____
_____
_____

Reflecting on my shining moments

1. _____

_____

_____

_____

_____

_____

2. _____

_____

_____

_____

_____

_____

3. _____

_____

_____

_____

_____

_____

Week: _____ Date: _____

Three shining moments of this day

1. _____

_____

_____

_____

_____

_____

2. _____

_____

_____

_____

_____

_____

3. _____

_____

_____

_____

_____

_____

Reflecting on my shining moments

1. _____

_____

_____

_____

_____

_____

2. _____

_____

_____

_____

_____

_____

3. _____

_____

_____

_____

_____

_____

Week: _____   Date: _____

Three shining moments of this day

1. _____

_____

_____

_____

_____

_____

2. _____

_____

_____

_____

_____

_____

3. _____

_____

_____

_____

_____

_____

Reflecting on my shining moments

1. _____

_____

_____

_____

_____

_____

_____

2. _____

_____

_____

_____

_____

_____

_____

3. _____

_____

_____

_____

_____

_____

_____

Bonus

Do something to express gratitude – describe what you did

_____

_____

_____

_____

_____

_____

_____

_____

_____

_____

_____

_____

_____

_____

_____

_____

_____

Reflection

How did it work, what did it mean, what did you learn,
how did you connect or inspire...

_____

_____

_____

_____

_____

_____

_____

_____

_____

_____

_____

_____

_____

_____

_____

_____

_____

_____

_____

Three shining moments of this day

1. _____

_____

_____

_____

_____

_____

_____

2. _____

_____

_____

_____

_____

_____

3. _____

_____

_____

_____

_____

_____

Reflecting on my shining moments

1. _____

_____

_____

_____

_____

_____

2. _____

_____

_____

_____

_____

_____

3. _____

_____

_____

_____

_____

_____

Week: _____ Date: _____

Three shining moments of this day

1. _____

_____

_____

_____

_____

_____

_____

2. _____

_____

_____

_____

_____

_____

_____

3. _____

_____

_____

_____

_____

_____

_____

Reflecting on my shining moments

1. _____

_____

_____

_____

_____

_____

2. _____

_____

_____

_____

_____

_____

3. _____

_____

_____

_____

_____

_____

Week: _____ Date: _____

Three shining moments of this day

1. _____

_____

_____

_____

_____

_____

2. _____

_____

_____

_____

_____

_____

3. _____

_____

_____

_____

_____

_____

Reflecting on my shining moments

1. _____

_____

_____

_____

_____

_____

2. _____

_____

_____

_____

_____

_____

3. _____

_____

_____

_____

_____

_____

Week: _____ Date: _____

Three shining moments of this day

1. _____

_____

_____

_____

_____

_____

_____

2. _____

_____

_____

_____

_____

_____

_____

3. _____

_____

_____

_____

_____

_____

Reflecting on my shining moments

1.

2.

3.

Week: _____ Date: _____

Three shining moments of this day

1. _____

_____

_____

_____

_____

_____

2. _____

_____

_____

_____

_____

_____

3. _____

_____

_____

_____

_____

_____

Reflecting on my shining moments

1. _____

_____

_____

_____

_____

_____

_____

2. _____

_____

_____

_____

_____

_____

_____

3. _____

_____

_____

_____

_____

_____

_____

Week: _____ Date: _____

Three shining moments of this day

1. _____

_____

_____

_____

_____

_____

2. _____

_____

_____

_____

_____

_____

3. _____

_____

_____

_____

_____

_____

Reflecting on my shining moments

1. _____

_____

_____

_____

_____

_____

2. _____

_____

_____

_____

_____

_____

3. _____

_____

_____

_____

_____

_____

Week: _____ Date: _____

Three shining moments of this day

1. _____

_____

_____

_____

_____

_____

2. _____

_____

_____

_____

_____

_____

3. _____

_____

_____

_____

_____

_____

Reflecting on my shining moments

1. _____

_____

_____

_____

_____

_____

2. _____

_____

_____

_____

_____

_____

3. _____

_____

_____

_____

_____

_____

Week: _____ Date: _____

Bonus

Do something to express gratitude – describe what you did

_____
_____
_____
_____
_____
_____
_____
_____
_____
_____
_____
_____
_____
_____
_____
_____
_____
_____
_____

Reflection

How did it work, what did it mean, what did you learn, how did you connect or inspire...

Week: _____   Date: _____

Three shining moments of this day

1. _____
_____
_____
_____
_____
_____

2. _____
_____
_____
_____
_____
_____

3. _____
_____
_____
_____
_____
_____

Reflecting on my shining moments

1. _____

_____

_____

_____

_____

_____

_____

2. _____

_____

_____

_____

_____

_____

_____

3. _____

_____

_____

_____

_____

_____

_____

Week: _____ Date: _____

Three shining moments of this day

1. _____
_____
_____
_____
_____
_____
_____

2. _____
_____
_____
_____
_____
_____
_____

3. _____
_____
_____
_____
_____
_____
_____

Reflecting on my shining moments

1. _____

_____

_____

_____

_____

_____

2. _____

_____

_____

_____

_____

_____

3. _____

_____

_____

_____

_____

_____

Week: _____ Date: _____

Three shining moments of this day

1. _____

_____

_____

_____

_____

_____

2. _____

_____

_____

_____

_____

_____

3. _____

_____

_____

_____

_____

_____

Reflecting on my shining moments

1.

2.

3.

Week: _____ Date: _____

Three shining moments of this day

1. _____
_____
_____
_____
_____
_____

2. _____
_____
_____
_____
_____
_____

3. _____
_____
_____
_____
_____

Reflecting on my shining moments

1. _____

_____

_____

_____

_____

_____

2. _____

_____

_____

_____

_____

_____

3. _____

_____

_____

_____

_____

_____

Week: _____ Date: _____

Three shining moments of this day

1. _____

_____

_____

_____

_____

_____

2. _____

_____

_____

_____

_____

_____

3. _____

_____

_____

_____

_____

_____

Reflecting on my shining moments

1. _____

_____

_____

_____

_____

_____

2. _____

_____

_____

_____

_____

_____

3. _____

_____

_____

_____

_____

_____

Week: _____ Date: _____

Three shining moments of this day

1. _____

_____

_____

_____

_____

_____

2. _____

_____

_____

_____

_____

_____

3. _____

_____

_____

_____

_____

_____

Reflecting on my shining moments

1. _____

_____

_____

_____

_____

_____

_____

2. _____

_____

_____

_____

_____

_____

_____

3. _____

_____

_____

_____

_____

_____

Week: _____ Date: _____

Three shining moments of this day

1. _____

_____

_____

_____

_____

_____

2. _____

_____

_____

_____

_____

_____

3. _____

_____

_____

_____

_____

_____

Reflecting on my shining moments

1. _____

_____

_____

_____

_____

_____

_____

2. _____

_____

_____

_____

_____

_____

_____

3. _____

_____

_____

_____

_____

_____

_____

Bonus

Do something to express gratitude – describe what you did

_____

_____

_____

_____

_____

_____

_____

_____

_____

_____

_____

_____

_____

_____

_____

_____

_____

_____

_____

_____

Reflection

How did it work, what did it mean, what did you learn,
how did you connect or inspire...

Week: _____ Date: _____

Three shining moments of this day

1. _____

_____

_____

_____

_____

_____

2. _____

_____

_____

_____

_____

_____

3. _____

_____

_____

_____

_____

_____

Reflecting on my shining moments

1. _____

_____

_____

_____

_____

_____

2. _____

_____

_____

_____

_____

_____

3. _____

_____

_____

_____

_____

_____

Week: _____ Date: _____

Three shining moments of this day

1. _____
_____
_____
_____
_____
_____

2. _____
_____
_____
_____
_____
_____

3. _____
_____
_____
_____
_____
_____

Reflecting on my shining moments

1. _____

_____

_____

_____

_____

_____

2. _____

_____

_____

_____

_____

_____

3. _____

_____

_____

_____

_____

_____

Week: _____ Date: _____

Three shining moments of this day

1. _____
   _____
   _____
   _____
   _____
   _____
   _____

2. _____
   _____
   _____
   _____
   _____
   _____
   _____

3. _____
   _____
   _____
   _____
   _____
   _____
   _____

Reflecting on my shining moments

1. _____

_____

_____

_____

_____

_____

2. _____

_____

_____

_____

_____

_____

3. _____

_____

_____

_____

_____

_____

Week: _____ Date: _____

Three shining moments of this day

1. _____

_____

_____

_____

_____

_____

2. _____

_____

_____

_____

_____

_____

3. _____

_____

_____

_____

_____

_____

Reflecting on my shining moments

1. _____

_____

_____

_____

_____

_____

_____

2. _____

_____

_____

_____

_____

_____

_____

3. _____

_____

_____

_____

_____

_____

_____

Week: _____ Date: _____

Three shining moments of this day

1. _____

_____

_____

_____

_____

_____

2. _____

_____

_____

_____

_____

_____

3. _____

_____

_____

_____

_____

_____

Reflecting on my shining moments

1. _____

_____

_____

_____

_____

_____

_____

2. _____

_____

_____

_____

_____

_____

_____

3. _____

_____

_____

_____

_____

_____

Week: _____ Date: _____

Three shining moments of this day

1. _____
   _____
   _____
   _____
   _____
   _____

2. _____
   _____
   _____
   _____
   _____
   _____

3. _____
   _____
   _____
   _____
   _____
   _____

Reflecting on my shining moments

1. _____

_____

_____

_____

_____

_____

_____

2. _____

_____

_____

_____

_____

_____

_____

3. _____

_____

_____

_____

_____

_____

_____

Week: _____ Date: _____

Three shining moments of this day

1. _____

   _____

   _____

   _____

   _____

   _____

2. _____

   _____

   _____

   _____

   _____

   _____

3. _____

   _____

   _____

   _____

   _____

   _____

Reflecting on my shining moments

1. _____

_____
_____
_____
_____
_____
_____

2. _____

_____
_____
_____
_____
_____
_____

3. _____

_____
_____
_____
_____
_____
_____

Bonus

Do something to express gratitude – describe what you did

_____
_____
_____
_____
_____
_____
_____
_____
_____
_____
_____
_____
_____
_____
_____
_____
_____
_____
_____

Reflection

How did it work, what did it mean, what did you learn, how did you connect or inspire...

_____

_____

_____

_____

_____

_____

_____

_____

_____

_____

_____

_____

_____

_____

_____

_____

_____

_____

Week: _____ Date: _____

Three shining moments of this day

1. _____

_____

_____

_____

_____

_____

2. _____

_____

_____

_____

_____

_____

3. _____

_____

_____

_____

_____

_____

Reflecting on my shining moments

1. _____

_____

_____

_____

_____

_____

2. _____

_____

_____

_____

_____

_____

3. _____

_____

_____

_____

_____

_____

Week: _____ Date: _____

Three shining moments of this day

1. _____

_____

_____

_____

_____

_____

2. _____

_____

_____

_____

_____

_____

3. _____

_____

_____

_____

_____

_____

Reflecting on my shining moments

1. _____

_____

_____

_____

_____

_____

2. _____

_____

_____

_____

_____

_____

3. _____

_____

_____

_____

_____

_____

Week: _____ Date: _____

Three shining moments of this day

1. _____
   _____
   _____
   _____
   _____
   _____

2. _____
   _____
   _____
   _____
   _____

3. _____
   _____
   _____
   _____
   _____

Reflecting on my shining moments

1. _____

_____

_____

_____

_____

_____

2. _____

_____

_____

_____

_____

_____

3. _____

_____

_____

_____

_____

_____

Week: _____ Date: _____

Three shining moments of this day

1. _____

_____

_____

_____

_____

_____

2. _____

_____

_____

_____

_____

_____

3. _____

_____

_____

_____

_____

_____

Reflecting on my shining moments

1. _____

_____

_____

_____

_____

_____

2. _____

_____

_____

_____

_____

_____

3. _____

_____

_____

_____

_____

_____

Week: _____ Date: _____

Three shining moments of this day

1. _____

_____

_____

_____

_____

_____

2. _____

_____

_____

_____

_____

_____

3. _____

_____

_____

_____

_____

_____

Reflecting on my shining moments

1.

2.

3.

Week: _____ Date: _____

Three shining moments of this day

1. _____

_____

_____

_____

_____

_____

2. _____

_____

_____

_____

_____

_____

3. _____

_____

_____

_____

_____

_____

Reflecting on my shining moments

1. _____

_____

_____

_____

_____

_____

2. _____

_____

_____

_____

_____

_____

3. _____

_____

_____

_____

_____

_____

Week: _____ Date: _____

Three shining moments of this day

1. _____

_____

_____

_____

_____

_____

2. _____

_____

_____

_____

_____

_____

3. _____

_____

_____

_____

_____

_____

Reflecting on my shining moments

1. _____

_____

_____

_____

_____

_____

2. _____

_____

_____

_____

_____

_____

3. _____

_____

_____

_____

_____

_____

Week: _____ Date: _____

Bonus

Do something to express gratitude – describe what you did

_____
_____
_____
_____
_____
_____
_____
_____
_____
_____
_____
_____
_____
_____
_____
_____
_____
_____
_____

Reflection

How did it work, what did it mean, what did you learn,
how did you connect or inspire...

Week: _____ Date: _____

Three shining moments of this day

1. _____

_____

_____

_____

_____

_____

2. _____

_____

_____

_____

_____

_____

3. _____

_____

_____

_____

_____

_____

Reflecting on my shining moments

1. _____

_____

_____

_____

_____

_____

2. _____

_____

_____

_____

_____

_____

3. _____

_____

_____

_____

_____

_____

Week: _____ Date: _____

Three shining moments of this day

1. _____
_____
_____
_____
_____
_____

2. _____
_____
_____
_____
_____
_____

3. _____
_____
_____
_____
_____
_____

Reflecting on my shining moments

1. _____

_____

_____

_____

_____

_____

2. _____

_____

_____

_____

_____

_____

3. _____

_____

_____

_____

_____

_____

Week: _____ Date: _____

Three shining moments of this day

1. _____
   _____
   _____
   _____
   _____
   _____

2. _____
   _____
   _____
   _____
   _____
   _____

3. _____
   _____
   _____
   _____
   _____
   _____

Reflecting on my shining moments

1. _____

_____

_____

_____

_____

_____

2. _____

_____

_____

_____

_____

_____

3. _____

_____

_____

_____

_____

_____

Week: _____ Date: _____

Three shining moments of this day

1. _____

_____

_____

_____

_____

_____

2. _____

_____

_____

_____

_____

_____

3. _____

_____

_____

_____

_____

_____

Reflecting on my shining moments

1. _____

_____

_____

_____

_____

_____

2. _____

_____

_____

_____

_____

_____

3. _____

_____

_____

_____

_____

_____

Week: _____ Date: _____

Three shining moments of this day

1. _____

_____

_____

_____

_____

_____

2. _____

_____

_____

_____

_____

_____

3. _____

_____

_____

_____

_____

_____

Reflecting on my shining moments

1. _____

_____

_____

_____

_____

_____

2. _____

_____

_____

_____

_____

_____

3. _____

_____

_____

_____

_____

_____

Week: _____ Date: _____

Three shining moments of this day

1. _____

   _____

   _____

   _____

   _____

2. _____

   _____

   _____

   _____

   _____

3. _____

   _____

   _____

   _____

   _____

Reflecting on my shining moments

1. _____

_____

_____

_____

_____

_____

2. _____

_____

_____

_____

_____

_____

3. _____

_____

_____

_____

_____

_____

Week: _____ Date: _____

Three shining moments of this day

1. _____

_____

_____

_____

_____

_____

_____

2. _____

_____

_____

_____

_____

_____

3. _____

_____

_____

_____

_____

_____

Reflecting on my shining moments

1. _____

_____

_____

_____

_____

_____

2. _____

_____

_____

_____

_____

_____

3. _____

_____

_____

_____

_____

_____

Week: _____ Date: _____

Bonus

Do something to express gratitude – describe what you did

_____
_____
_____
_____
_____
_____
_____
_____
_____
_____
_____
_____
_____
_____
_____
_____
_____
_____

Reflection

How did it work, what did it mean, what did you learn, how did you connect or inspire...

Week: _____ Date: _____

Three shining moments of this day

1. _____

_____

_____

_____

_____

_____

2. _____

_____

_____

_____

_____

_____

3. _____

_____

_____

_____

_____

_____

Reflecting on my shining moments

1. _____
_____
_____
_____
_____
_____

2. _____
_____
_____
_____
_____
_____

3. _____
_____
_____
_____
_____
_____

Week: _____ Date: _____

Three shining moments of this day

1. _____

_____

_____

_____

_____

_____

2. _____

_____

_____

_____

_____

3. _____

_____

_____

_____

_____

_____

Reflecting on my shining moments

1. _____

_____

_____

_____

_____

_____

2. _____

_____

_____

_____

_____

_____

3. _____

_____

_____

_____

_____

_____

Week: _____ Date: _____

Three shining moments of this day

1. _____

_____

_____

_____

_____

_____

2. _____

_____

_____

_____

_____

3. _____

_____

_____

_____

_____

_____

Reflecting on my shining moments

1.
_____

_____

_____

_____

_____

_____

_____

2.
_____

_____

_____

_____

_____

_____

_____

3.
_____

_____

_____

_____

_____

_____

_____

Week: _____ Date: _____

Three shining moments of this day

1. _____
_____
_____
_____
_____
_____

2. _____
_____
_____
_____
_____
_____

3. _____
_____
_____
_____
_____
_____

Reflecting on my shining moments

1. _____

_____

_____

_____

_____

_____

_____

2. _____

_____

_____

_____

_____

_____

_____

3. _____

_____

_____

_____

_____

_____

_____

Week: _____ Date: _____

Three shining moments of this day

1. _____
_____
_____
_____
_____
_____

2. _____
_____
_____
_____
_____
_____

3. _____
_____
_____
_____
_____
_____

Reflecting on my shining moments

1. _____

_____

_____

_____

_____

_____

_____

2. _____

_____

_____

_____

_____

_____

_____

3. _____

_____

_____

_____

_____

_____

_____

Week: _____ Date: _____

Three shining moments of this day

1. _____
_____
_____
_____
_____
_____

2. _____
_____
_____
_____
_____
_____

3. _____
_____
_____
_____
_____
_____

Reflecting on my shining moments

1. _____
   _____
   _____
   _____
   _____
   _____
   _____

2. _____
   _____
   _____
   _____
   _____
   _____

3. _____
   _____
   _____
   _____
   _____
   _____

Week: _____ Date: _____

Three shining moments of this day

1. _____
_____
_____
_____
_____
_____

2. _____
_____
_____
_____
_____

3. _____
_____
_____
_____
_____

Reflecting on my shining moments

1.
_____

_____

_____

_____

_____

_____

2.
_____

_____

_____

_____

_____

3.
_____

_____

_____

_____

_____

Week: _____ Date: _____

Bonus

Do something to express gratitude – describe what you did

_____
_____
_____
_____
_____
_____
_____
_____
_____
_____
_____
_____
_____
_____
_____
_____
_____
_____
_____
_____

Reflection

How did it work, what did it mean, what did you learn,
how did you connect or inspire...

Week: _____ Date: _____

Three shining moments of this day

1. _____

_____

_____

_____

_____

_____

2. _____

_____

_____

_____

_____

_____

3. _____

_____

_____

_____

_____

_____

Reflecting on my shining moments

1. _____

2. _____

3. _____

Week: _____ Date: _____

Three shining moments of this day

1. _____
   _____
   _____
   _____
   _____
   _____

2. _____
   _____
   _____
   _____
   _____
   _____

3. _____
   _____
   _____
   _____
   _____
   _____

Reflecting on my shining moments

1. _____
   _____
   _____
   _____
   _____
   _____
   _____

2. _____
   _____
   _____
   _____
   _____
   _____

3. _____
   _____
   _____
   _____
   _____
   _____

Week: _____ Date: _____

Three shining moments of this day

1. _____
_____
_____
_____
_____
_____

2. _____
_____
_____
_____
_____
_____

3. _____
_____
_____
_____
_____
_____

Reflecting on my shining moments

1. _____
_____
_____
_____
_____
_____
_____

2. _____
_____
_____
_____
_____
_____
_____

3. _____
_____
_____
_____
_____
_____
_____

Week: _____   Date: _____

Three shining moments of this day

1. _____

_____

_____

_____

_____

_____

2. _____

_____

_____

_____

_____

_____

3. _____

_____

_____

_____

_____

_____

Reflecting on my shining moments

1.
_____

_____

_____

_____

_____

_____

2.
_____

_____

_____

_____

_____

3.
_____

_____

_____

_____

_____

_____

Week: _____ Date: _____

Three shining moments of this day

1. _____

_____

_____

_____

_____

_____

2. _____

_____

_____

_____

_____

_____

3. _____

_____

_____

_____

_____

_____

Reflecting on my shining moments

1.

2.

3.

Week: _____ Date: _____

Three shining moments of this day

1. _____
_____
_____
_____
_____
_____
_____

2. _____
_____
_____
_____
_____
_____
_____

3. _____
_____
_____
_____
_____
_____
_____

Reflecting on my shining moments

1. _____

_____

_____

_____

_____

_____

2. _____

_____

_____

_____

_____

3. _____

_____

_____

_____

_____

Week: _____ Date: _____

Three shining moments of this day

1. _____
   _____
   _____
   _____
   _____
   _____

2. _____
   _____
   _____
   _____
   _____

3. _____
   _____
   _____
   _____
   _____

Reflecting on my shining moments

1. _____

_____

_____

_____

_____

_____

_____

2. _____

_____

_____

_____

_____

_____

3. _____

_____

_____

_____

_____

_____

Week: _____ Date: _____

Bonus

Do something to express gratitude – describe what
you did

_____
_____
_____
_____
_____
_____
_____
_____
_____
_____
_____
_____
_____
_____
_____
_____
_____
_____
_____

Reflection

How did it work, what did it mean, what did you learn, how did you connect or inspire...

Week: _____ Date: _____

Three shining moments of this day

1. _____

_____

_____

_____

_____

_____

2. _____

_____

_____

_____

_____

_____

3. _____

_____

_____

_____

_____

_____

Reflecting on my shining moments

1.
_____
_____
_____
_____
_____
_____
_____

2.
_____
_____
_____
_____
_____
_____
_____

3.
_____
_____
_____
_____
_____
_____
_____

Week: _____   Date: _____

Three shining moments of this day

1. _____

_____

_____

_____

_____

_____

2. _____

_____

_____

_____

_____

_____

3. _____

_____

_____

_____

_____

_____

Reflecting on my shining moments

1. _____

_____

_____

_____

_____

_____

2. _____

_____

_____

_____

_____

3. _____

_____

_____

_____

_____

Week: _____ Date: _____

Three shining moments of this day

1. _____
   _____
   _____
   _____
   _____
   _____

2. _____
   _____
   _____
   _____
   _____
   _____

3. _____
   _____
   _____
   _____
   _____
   _____

Reflecting on my shining moments

1. _____

_____

_____

_____

_____

_____

_____

2. _____

_____

_____

_____

_____

_____

_____

3. _____

_____

_____

_____

_____

_____

_____

Week: _____ Date: _____

Three shining moments of this day

1. _____
_____
_____
_____
_____
_____

2. _____
_____
_____
_____
_____
_____

3. _____
_____
_____
_____
_____
_____

Reflecting on my shining moments

1.

2.

3.

Week: _____ Date: _____

Three shining moments of this day

1. _____
   _____
   _____
   _____
   _____
   _____

2. _____
   _____
   _____
   _____
   _____
   _____

3. _____
   _____
   _____
   _____
   _____
   _____

Reflecting on my shining moments

1. _____

2. _____

3. _____

Week: _____   Date: _____

Three shining moments of this day

1. _____
_____
_____
_____
_____
_____

2. _____
_____
_____
_____
_____
_____

3. _____
_____
_____
_____
_____
_____

Reflecting on my shining moments

1.
_____
_____
_____
_____
_____
_____
_____

2.
_____
_____
_____
_____
_____
_____
_____

3.
_____
_____
_____
_____
_____
_____
_____

Week: _____ Date: _____

Three shining moments of this day

1. _____
_____
_____
_____
_____
_____

2. _____
_____
_____
_____
_____
_____

3. _____
_____
_____
_____
_____
_____

Reflecting on my shining moments

1.

2.

3.

Bonus

Do something to express gratitude – describe what
you did

_____

_____

_____

_____

_____

_____

_____

_____

_____

_____

_____

_____

_____

_____

_____

_____

_____

Reflection

How did it work, what did it mean, what did you learn,
how did you connect or inspire...

_____

_____

_____

_____

_____

_____

_____

_____

_____

_____

_____

_____

_____

_____

_____

_____

_____

_____

_____

_____

Week: _____ Date: _____

Three shining moments of this day

1. _____

_____

_____

_____

_____

_____

2. _____

_____

_____

_____

_____

3. _____

_____

_____

_____

_____

_____

Reflecting on my shining moments

1.

2.

3.

Week: _____   Date: _____

Three shining moments of this day

1. _____
_____
_____
_____
_____
_____

2. _____
_____
_____
_____
_____
_____

3. _____
_____
_____
_____
_____
_____

Reflecting on my shining moments

Week: _____ Date: _____

Three shining moments of this day

1. _____

_____

_____

_____

_____

_____

2. _____

_____

_____

_____

_____

3. _____

_____

_____

_____

_____

_____

Reflecting on my shining moments

1. _____

2. _____

3. _____

Week: _____ Date: _____

Three shining moments of this day

1. _____

_____

_____

_____

_____

_____

2. _____

_____

_____

_____

_____

_____

3. _____

_____

_____

_____

_____

_____

Reflecting on my shining moments

1. _____

_____

_____

_____

_____

_____

_____

2. _____

_____

_____

_____

_____

_____

_____

3. _____

_____

_____

_____

_____

_____

_____

Week: _____ Date: _____

Three shining moments of this day

1. _____

_____

_____

_____

_____

_____

2. _____

_____

_____

_____

_____

_____

3. _____

_____

_____

_____

_____

_____

Reflecting on my shining moments

1. _____

_____

_____

_____

_____

_____

_____

2. _____

_____

_____

_____

_____

_____

_____

3. _____

_____

_____

_____

_____

_____

_____

Week: _____ Date: _____

Three shining moments of this day

1. _____
_____
_____
_____
_____
_____

2. _____
_____
_____
_____
_____

3. _____
_____
_____
_____
_____

Reflecting on my shining moments

1.

2.

3.

Week: _____ Date: _____

Three shining moments of this day

1. _____

_____

_____

_____

_____

_____

2. _____

_____

_____

_____

_____

_____

3. _____

_____

_____

_____

_____

_____

Reflecting on my shining moments

Bonus

Do something to express gratitude – describe what you did

_____

_____

_____

_____

_____

_____

_____

_____

_____

_____

_____

_____

_____

_____

_____

_____

_____

_____

_____

Reflection

How did it work, what did it mean, what did you learn,
how did you connect or inspire...

_____

_____

_____

_____

_____

_____

_____

_____

_____

_____

_____

_____

_____

_____

_____

_____

_____

_____

_____

_____

_____

Week: _____   Date: _____

Three shining moments of this day

1. _____
_____
_____
_____
_____
_____
_____

2. _____
_____
_____
_____
_____
_____
_____

3. _____
_____
_____
_____
_____
_____

Reflecting on my shining moments

Week: _____   Date: _____

Three shining moments of this day

1. _____

_____

_____

_____

_____

_____

2. _____

_____

_____

_____

_____

_____

3. _____

_____

_____

_____

_____

_____

Reflecting on my shining moments

1. _____

_____

_____

_____

_____

_____

2. _____

_____

_____

_____

_____

3. _____

_____

_____

_____

_____

Week: _____   Date: _____

Three shining moments of this day

1. _____
   _____
   _____
   _____
   _____
   _____

2. _____
   _____
   _____
   _____
   _____
   _____

3. _____
   _____
   _____
   _____
   _____
   _____

Reflecting on my shining moments

1. _____
_____
_____
_____
_____
_____
_____

2. _____
_____
_____
_____
_____
_____
_____

3. _____
_____
_____
_____
_____
_____
_____

Week: _____   Date: _____

Three shining moments of this day

1. _____
   _____
   _____
   _____
   _____
   _____

2. _____
   _____
   _____
   _____
   _____
   _____

3. _____
   _____
   _____
   _____
   _____
   _____

Reflecting on my shining moments

Week: _____ Date: _____

Three shining moments of this day

1. _____
_____
_____
_____
_____
_____
_____

2. _____
_____
_____
_____
_____
_____

3. _____
_____
_____
_____
_____
_____

Reflecting on my shining moments

_____

_____

_____

_____

_____

_____

_____

_____

_____

_____

_____

_____

_____

_____

_____

_____

_____

_____

Week: _____ Date: _____

Three shining moments of this day

1. _____
   _____
   _____
   _____
   _____
   _____

2. _____
   _____
   _____
   _____
   _____
   _____

3. _____
   _____
   _____
   _____
   _____
   _____

Reflecting on my shining moments

1.

2.

3.

Week: _____ Date: _____

Three shining moments of this day

1. _____
   _____
   _____
   _____
   _____
   _____

2. _____
   _____
   _____
   _____
   _____
   _____

3. _____
   _____
   _____
   _____
   _____
   _____

Reflecting on my shining moments

1. _____

_____

_____

_____

_____

_____

_____

2. _____

_____

_____

_____

_____

_____

_____

3. _____

_____

_____

_____

_____

_____

_____

Bonus

Do something to express gratitude − describe what
you did

_____

_____

_____

_____

_____

_____

_____

_____

_____

_____

_____

_____

_____

_____

_____

_____

_____

_____

Reflection

How did it work, what did it mean, what did you learn, how did you connect or inspire...

_____

_____

_____

_____

_____

_____

_____

_____

_____

_____

_____

_____

_____

_____

_____

_____

_____

_____

_____

Week: _____ Date: _____

Three shining moments of this day

1. _____

_____

_____

_____

_____

_____

2. _____

_____

_____

_____

_____

_____

3. _____

_____

_____

_____

_____

_____

Reflecting on my shining moments

1.
_____
_____
_____
_____
_____
_____
_____

2.
_____
_____
_____
_____
_____
_____
_____

3.
_____
_____
_____
_____
_____
_____
_____

Week: _____ Date: _____

Three shining moments of this day

1. _____

_____

_____

_____

_____

_____

2. _____

_____

_____

_____

_____

_____

3. _____

_____

_____

_____

_____

_____

Reflecting on my shining moments

1. _____

_____

_____

_____

_____

_____

_____

2. _____

_____

_____

_____

_____

_____

_____

3. _____

_____

_____

_____

_____

_____

_____

Week: _____ Date: _____

Three shining moments of this day

1. _____

_____

_____

_____

_____

_____

2. _____

_____

_____

_____

_____

_____

3. _____

_____

_____

_____

_____

_____

Reflecting on my shining moments

1. _____

_____

_____

_____

_____

_____

_____

2. _____

_____

_____

_____

_____

_____

_____

3. _____

_____

_____

_____

_____

_____

_____

Week: _____   Date: _____

Three shining moments of this day

1. _____

_____

_____

_____

_____

_____

2. _____

_____

_____

_____

_____

_____

3. _____

_____

_____

_____

_____

_____

Reflecting on my shining moments

1.

2.

3.

Week: _____ Date: _____

Three shining moments of this day

1. _____
_____
_____
_____
_____
_____

2. _____
_____
_____
_____
_____
_____

3. _____
_____
_____
_____
_____
_____

Reflecting on my shining moments

1. _____

_____

_____

_____

_____

_____

_____

2. _____

_____

_____

_____

_____

_____

3. _____

_____

_____

_____

_____

_____

Week: _____ Date: _____

Three shining moments of this day

1. _____
_____
_____
_____
_____
_____

2. _____
_____
_____
_____
_____
_____

3. _____
_____
_____
_____
_____
_____

Reflecting on my shining moments

Week: _____ Date: _____

Three shining moments of this day

1. _____

_____

_____

_____

_____

_____

2. _____

_____

_____

_____

_____

_____

3. _____

_____

_____

_____

_____

_____

Reflecting on my shining moments

- ---

- ---

Bonus

Do something to express gratitude – describe what you did

_____

_____

_____

_____

_____

_____

_____

_____

_____

_____

_____

_____

_____

_____

_____

_____

_____

_____

_____

Reflection

How did it work, what did it mean, what did you learn,
how did you connect or inspire...

Week: _____ Date: _____

Three shining moments of this day

1. _____

_____

_____

_____

_____

_____

2. _____

_____

_____

_____

_____

_____

3. _____

_____

_____

_____

_____

_____

Reflecting on my shining moments

Week: _____ Date: _____

Three shining moments of this day

1. _____

_____

_____

_____

_____

_____

2. _____

_____

_____

_____

_____

_____

3. _____

_____

_____

_____

_____

_____

Reflecting on my shining moments

Week: _____ Date: _____

Three shining moments of this day

1. _____
_____
_____
_____
_____
_____

2. _____
_____
_____
_____
_____
_____

3. _____
_____
_____
_____
_____
_____

Reflecting on my shining moments

1.

2.

3.

Week: _____ Date: _____

Three shining moments of this day

1. _____
   _____
   _____
   _____
   _____
   _____

2. _____
   _____
   _____
   _____
   _____
   _____

3. _____
   _____
   _____
   _____
   _____
   _____

Reflecting on my shining moments

·   _____

_____

_____

_____

_____

_____

_____

·   _____

_____

_____

_____

_____

_____

_____

·   _____

_____

_____

_____

_____

_____

_____

Week: _____ Date: _____

Three shining moments of this day

1. _____

_____

_____

_____

_____

2. _____

_____

_____

_____

_____

3. _____

_____

_____

_____

_____

Reflecting on my shining moments

Week: _____ Date: _____

Three shining moments of this day

1. _____
   _____
   _____
   _____
   _____
   _____
   _____

2. _____
   _____
   _____
   _____
   _____
   _____
   _____

3. _____
   _____
   _____
   _____
   _____
   _____
   _____

Reflecting on my shining moments

Week: _____ Date: _____

Three shining moments of this day

1. _____
   _____
   _____
   _____
   _____
   _____
   _____

2. _____
   _____
   _____
   _____
   _____
   _____
   _____

3. _____
   _____
   _____
   _____
   _____
   _____

Reflecting on my shining moments

1. _____

_____

_____

_____

_____

_____

_____

2. _____

_____

_____

_____

_____

_____

3. _____

_____

_____

_____

_____

_____

_____

Made in the USA
Monee, IL
18 November 2022